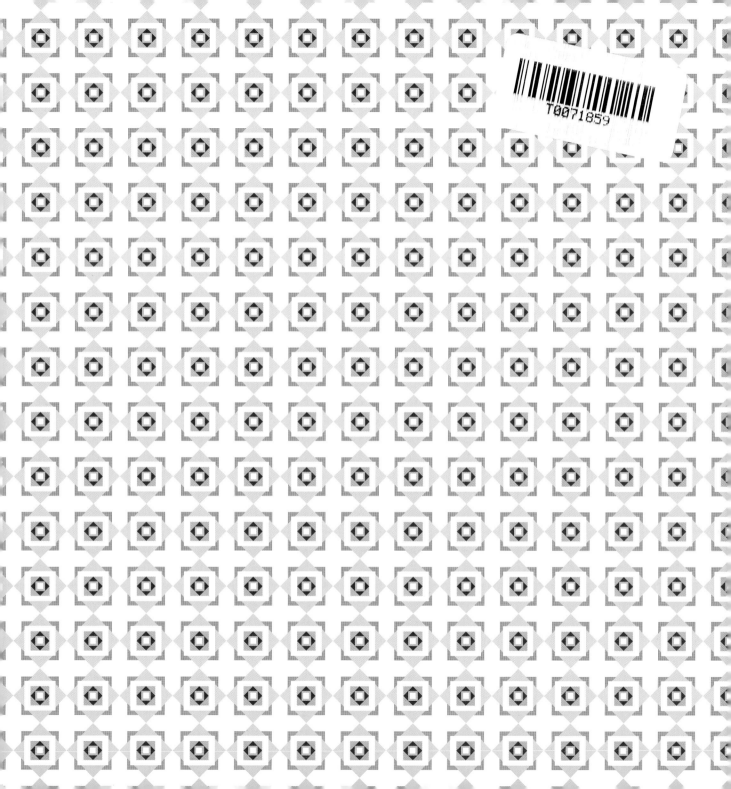

Skyhorse Publishing books may be purchased in bulk at special discounts for sales promotion, corporate gifts, fund-raising, or educational purposes. Special editions can also be created to specifications. For details, contact the Special Sales Department, Skyhorse Publishing, 307 West 36th Street, 11th Floor, New York, NY 10018 or info@skyhorsepublishing.com.

Skyhorse® and Skyhorse Publishing® are registered trademarks of Skyhorse Publishing, Inc.®, a Delaware corporation.

www.skyhorsepublishing.com

10 9 8 7 6 5 4 3 2 1

Library of Congress Cataloging-in-Publication Data is available on file.

Cover design by Eric Kang

Print ISBN: 978-1-63220-366-3
Ebook ISBN 978-1-63450-108-8

Printed in China

Creating with Concrete & Mosaic

Fun and Decorative Ideas for Your Home and Garden

Sania Hedengren & Susanna Zacke

Photography by Magnus Selander

Translated by Ellen Hedström

Skyhorse Publishing

SANIA   SUSANNA

" susanna likes pink and red

sania likes yellow and green "

WE WOULD LIKE TO THANK EVERYONE
WHO HAS BEEN INVOLVED WITH THIS BOOK.

Our helpful husbands, Michael and P-G, who proofread, searched for typefaces, carried things, and fixed a lot of other practical items.

Finja Betong, who provided us with concrete!

Raja, Tabbouli House, Franska Kakelbutiken (the French tile company), and Panduro craft store, who lent us props.

Our children, Pontus, Nicole, Elin, Lisa, and Hanna, who endured the mess at home during photo shoots.

Everyone who owns our first book, *Concrete Crafts*. Because there are so many of you, we decided to create another book.

Eva and Annelie (and everyone else) at our favorite Swedish publisher, Semic. Thank you, as always, for the great collaboration!

Last but not least, our photographer Magnus Selander, who creates such beautiful images of our work.
He manages to work with impossible angles, our constant demands, and difficult lighting to produce the best images. Nothing is impossible for this man!

Contents

Creating with Concrete & Mosaic

Here it is, our second book about concrete, an awesome material that we never tire of. If you already read our first book, you'll find many new casting ideas, and if you're a beginner, you might as well start here. We just want to continue sharing our ideas and the joy we experience from creating things with concrete.

It's not difficult to cast your own creations. You can easily make professional-looking items from concrete in a day. In this book, we have also chosen to use tiles, mosaic, and crushed porcelain in some of the projects. They are both super fun and very easy to use and incredibly beautiful when combined with concrete. Some projects are purely concrete based, others are completely mosaic based, and some are a combination of both.

To cast in concrete you simply mix fine concrete with water and then pour it into molds of various shapes and sizes. The main thing is to use your imagination when looking for molds. An old rubber boot or a cake tin are examples of molds that you probably already have at home. You can even build your own molds if you want to make a tabletop, for example. The variations are endless.

You can add mosaics to almost anything. The old table in the garage or a thrift store mirror are given a new spark of life and a unique look if you dress them in mosaic. Tile adhesive and grout is all you need—and the mosaic of course. The availability of tiles and mosaic is enormous; beautiful Moroccan ceramic tiles, antique tiles from India, or white modern circular mosaics are all examples of things we like. You can also create a great look by crushing some old porcelain and using the shards to make mosaics.

This book contains a wide variety of projects from the unique mosaic ring to concrete stairs, and everything in-between. Super easy or a bit more advanced, there is something for everyone here. So be inspired and let your creativity flow, and good luck!

Sania and Susanna

A Guide to
CONCRETE

WHAT IS CONCRETE?

Concrete consists of 80 percent ballast rock, which is comprised of sand, stone, and gravel; 14 percent cement, which consists of heated and ground limestone; and 6 percent water. Therefore, concrete is a natural material that is eco-friendly, useful, and long lasting. With a long history of usage, concrete is one of the world's most important building materials. Ancient buildings, such as amphitheatres, bridges, and houses, that have been built using concrete have been around since the second or third century. The fine concrete that we have used is usually quite smooth because it contains small stones that are a maximum of 1/8 inches (4 mm) in size. If you prefer concrete that is even smoother, you can find various concrete repair products at your local home improvement center.

MOLDS

Your choice of mold is the most important thing when working with concrete, as this is what delivers your result. This part requires a bit of creative thinking. Plastic is a great choice because it's elastic and has a smooth surface that can be easily removed. However, other materials such as strong cardboard, wood, or rubber and silicon also work well. If you brush the inside of the mold with vegetable oil, the concrete will be easier to release from the mold. Buckets, plastic pots, and old packaging are examples of good, cheap molds.

Sometimes you might have to cut the mold to release the concrete, so the cheaper the material, the better. You can even get a little more creative—an old rubber boot, a plastic ball, or a silicon muffin tray can make unique and wonderful creations. Keep your eyes open for unusual shapes in thrift stores and yard sales, as these places can be a real goldmine for cheap molds!

For tabletops and other furniture you will need to make a frame from particleboard and joists. An alternative to particleboard is form plywood, a smooth water-resistant board that is made especially for casting in concrete. Because they are waterproof, they can be reused. It is a bit more expensive, but can be a worthy investment if you plan to make more advanced projects. Form plywood is made so that it does not stick to the concrete. The benefit of building your own mold is that you can customize it to your desired size.

REINFORCEMENT

Reinforcing the concrete is necessary when making larger pieces. A tabletop, for example, needs to be strengthened so it doesn't break. Reinforcing also makes the concrete more resistant to freezing temperatures. It's not as complicated as it sounds. To reinforce concrete, you can use rebar, reinforcement mesh, chicken wire, or galvanized wire mesh. The latter two are softer and easy to cut using a pair of pliers. If you use reinforcing bars or mesh, it will be cut at the home improvement center, where the tools required are available. If you are making larger projects, we suggest you ask an expert for more advice on reinforcing to acheive the right dimensions.

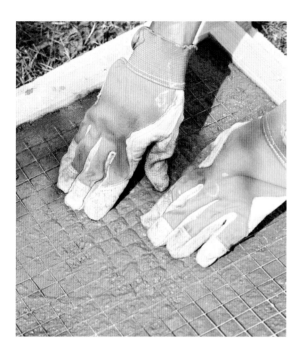

To reinforce a project, cut a piece to fit the mold. Press the mesh into the wet concrete, and if necessary add some more concrete to keep it in place. It is important that the reinforcement sits in the "middle" of the concrete.

DECORATION

Your imagination is the only limitation when it comes to decorating concrete. It is a very forgiving material to work with as you can merely "press" whatever you want to decorate with into the wet concrete. Mosaic, tiles, and ceramic tiles all add character to the concrete and you can either cast straight into the concrete or press the mosaic into it. Pretty, colorful buttons are also examples of decorations that can turn a plant pot into a work of art. If you want to create an irregular pattern using homemade mosaic, you can crush some old chipped porcelain. Mix different patterns and colors. Old porcelain is easy to find at thrift stores for next to nothing. Giving the concrete a pattern also leads to very impressive results. Textiles, plastic, paper, Styrofoam, and rubber are great materials that work well as patterns. Wallpaper with a raised plastic pattern and small, crocheted tablecloths are both perfect to cast on.

WAITING TIME

"Curing" refers to the process of drying, hardening, and solidfying. The length of time this takes varies depending on the thickness and size of the item cast, but expect to wait at least a day or two. It is important that the concrete is on a flat surface so that it remains even. Tabletops are a great example of something that really need to lie flat, so plan in advance where you are going to leave your items to dry—preferably in a shady and cool place. It is a good idea to cover the item with plastic—a bag, plastic wrap, or a tarp. To make the concrete cure more slowly, spray it with water a few times using a spray bottle while it's curing. It requires a lot of patience and more likely than not you will be curious to see the results, but don't remove the item too quickly, as you will risk breaking it. Try and hold out for at least 24 hours!

" We still love browsing through yard sales and thrift stores. There's nothing more exciting! We love finding fun items to cover with mosaics—tables, chairs, trays . . . "

For smaller items you can easily mix the concrete in a small bowl with a spoon.
For larger projects, mix concrete with water in a bucket. A whisk attached to a drill or screwdriver makes this heavy work a bit lighter.

MIXING CONCRETE

When you've planned and prepared your molds for casting, it's time to mix your concrete. All you need is water and some fine concrete that is mixed together into a batter. These instructions are the same for everything you choose to make.

YOU WILL NEED:

- Fine concrete. This can be found in home improvement centers in approximately 55 lb (25 kg) bags.
- One or more plastic bucket to mix in.
- Water.
- A spade or trowel to mix with. A whisk attached to a screwdriver or drill makes it a bit easier.
- Gloves. Concrete is quite corrosive and dries the skin out.
- Mask. Avoid inhaling concrete dust.

Start by pouring a small amount of water into a bucket and then add the concrete powder (read the proportions for water/concrete on the packaging). It's quite easy to mix concrete using common sense, especially if you are only mixing a small amount. Stir, whisk, and mix carefully with a spade or whisk—if you are making a whole bucketful we recommend a whisk—until the consistency resembles thick porridge. It's that simple to make and now you are ready to start casting.

Estimating the exact amount of concrete for each different project is impossible, as it depends on what you are making and how big the mold is. A bucket of mixed concrete is enough to make two average-sized pots. Mix the concrete as you cast, one bucket at a time. Don't let the mixture stand for too long or it will start to set. Clean your tools immediately; as dried concrete is impossible to remove, we recommend having a watering can or hose close by.

Working outdoors is best, as it can get quite messy when you cast—a balcony works well too. Don't cast things in the winter though, as wet concrete can't take cold weather. If you want to make smaller projects indoors, that's fine as long as you have a good surface to work on and remember to cover the floors. Also be sure to work carefully so you do not get dust everywhere. This way you can make small pots, bowls, pot holders, and so on.

A Guide to
MOSAIC

A BIT OF HISTORY

The earliest known mosaics are at least 5,000 years old. "Mosaic" means a decorative combination of small pieces in different colors that create a pattern or image. The materials can be porcelain, stone, or glass, which should be affixed to a hard surface. Floor mosaics with abstract patterns are the oldest known types and probably served the same purpose as carpets these days. Many mosaics from the Roman Empire are still intact and some of the most exquisite ones can be found in Roman churches. The Pope was ordering mosaics to cover walls, floors, and ceilings as early as the 9th century.

In our home country of Sweden, there are several known mosaics from the 20th century, for example in the city hall in Stockholm, cathedrals in Linköping and Lund, and in Kila church near Nyköping. These days, mosaics are more often found in public places, such as the subways stations in Stockholm.

OUR MOSAIC

For the projects in this book, we have used tiles, ceramics, and "mosaic materials." We consider "mosaic materials" to be anything from colorful buttons to glass beads and more regular mosaic tiles found in stores. The variations are endless and it's all about your own preference and style as well as imagination. By decorating with mosaic, you can make old things into completely new creations that are unique and personal. Tables, mirrors, chairs, and pots can all be covered with mosaic.

Odd bits of porcelain can also be used. Place a piece of porcelain in a towel or wrap in newspaper and bang it lightly with a hammer. Use the shards to make decorative mosaics. Tiles can be divided the same way; all you have to do is indulge in a variety of colors, mixing and creating patterns.

Personally we think the combination of concrete and mosaic is a match made in heaven; the concrete's light gray, slightly rough surface works really well with the colorful mosaic. Gently press or tap the pieces into the wet concrete for a simple but very striking result.

WORKING WITH MOSAIC

All you really need for this are two things—apart from the mosaic itself—tile adhesive and grout, which you can find in a craft store or home improvement centers. The surface that is being covered needs to be clean and dry. The glue is painted onto the surface with an adhesive comb spreader. Place the mosaic, tiles, or shards in the pattern you want. It is a good idea to test the pattern out before gluing so you can see what it looks like and make sure the measurements work. A tile nipper can be useful to cut the mosaic bits to size. When the glue is dry, it is time to grout. Mix the grout according to the instructions on the packet and brush it over the tiles/mosaic with the grout spreader. Wipe away any excess with a damp sponge and when it's dry, polish the surface with a dry cloth. Grout is available in many different colors, but we prefer white so the grout in our projects is always white.

Super easy is what we call the projects that are so easy that it's hard to fail. That doesn't mean that the results look simple or cheap. Oftentimes the simplest things look the best.

Sometimes the result can even look more advanced than it really is, which is great. Make some jewelry, dress a table, or decorate your garden, all with concrete and mosaic.

The Rose AT THE DOOR

Casting in concrete is like baking, but with a heavier batter; for this project this certainly rings true. This doorstop is cast in a cake tin. It really is as simple as that. While we were at it we made some muffins too!

- Brush the inside of the mold with vegetable oil.
- Mix the concrete according to the instructions on page 12.
- Pour the concrete into the mold.
- Gently tap the mold against the ground a few times to remove any air bubbles.
- Leave the concrete to dry for at least 24 hours in a shady area.
- For the best results, water the concrete a few times while it is drying.
- Remove the rose from the mold.
- Place the concrete rose by the door as a doorstop. The small roses can be used as decorations, inside or outside.

Basic silicon cake and muffin tins are perfect for casting in concrete. We bought these in a department store and they can be used again and again.

Fill the mold with concrete, just as if you were making a cake. When the mold is filled, tap it lightly against the ground to remove air bubbles so that the surface is smooth. Now leave the concrete to dry for 24 hours.

The large rose is perfect as a doorstop and it's decorative and practical at the same time. The rose gets a nice surface from the soft muffin tin, which is perfect for casting in.

The roses that were cast in the muffin tin make cute decorative pieces for the window. Place several of them in a row for the best effect.

MOSAIC ON YOUR *Finger*

Isn't it great? This mosaic ring is so easy to make. Look for really pretty pieces of mosaic at the tile store. There are lots to choose from. From handmade and patterned tiles to more simple smooth ones, the color choices are endless.

Buying a couple individual pieces of mosaic tiles, or even a single sheet, doesn't have to be expensive, even if the square foot price is quite high. Make several rings in different colors and designs and you can match them to your outfits.

- You need a ring, which you can find in a craft store.
- Glue the mosaic onto the ring using really strong glue. Ask the store associates what they recommend.
- Leave it to dry completely.
- Your ring is finished.

A piece of mosaic is glued onto a ring with super glue and left to dry.

Your ring is unique and personal and much better value than diamonds!

A CONCRETE *Boot*

Sometimes you make stuff just for fun, and making a concrete boot is one of these instances. It really has no use but it is super fun to make. If you have spare old boots at home, use those; if not, buy a cheap pair. Old boots your children have grown out of are also good to use.

The boot has to be cut up when it is time to remove the concrete. Seeing the smooth concrete boot with its perfect shape appear is quite exciting.

The boot will definitely be eye-catching in the backyard.

- Try to remove any lining in the boot.
- Mix the concrete according to the instructions on page 12.
- Fill the whole boot with concrete, all the way up to the top.
- Gently tap the boot against the ground a few times to remove any air bubbles. This will leave the surface of the concrete smooth.
- Leave the boot to dry for at least 24 hours, avoiding sunshine.
- Cut up the rubber boot to remove the concrete.
- The boot is ready to be placed in the garden, although it is just as fun to keep indoors. Maybe it will make a great present for that person who already has everything . . .

"Worth remembering when casting—the inside becomes the surface (in most cases)."

It's fun and slightly crazy to fill a
rubber boot with concrete.

The concrete boot has a beautiful
shape and a smooth surface,
which catches everyone's eye.

AS CLEAR AS *Glass*

Your glasses definitely need coasters, and using these attractive tiles gives your table an edgy feel. Choose your favorite tiles or match the coasters to the tiles in the kitchen. There are many alternatives to choose from and they can be created quickly. If you don't want too many coasters, you can just make one that can be used for a vase of flowers.

- Collect the number of tiles you need; you can often buy odd tiles on their own at a low cost.
- Place felt pads underneath to protect the surface of the table.
- Place the coasters on the table.

The felt pads protect the table-top from being scratched, as the tiles are often a bit rough underneath.

We instantly fell for these handmade tiles from France, which we chose to make our coasters from.

We quickly created a beautiful arrangement for the table using a patterned tile from India and some peonies in a vase.

A PRETTY *Vase*

A basic cylinder shaped glass vase can be made into something so decorative that you won't need to add flowers. We added small flowers to this vase, using glass beads with a flat side so that it was easy to attach them.

Scour the craft stores for pretty beads, then all you have to do is get gluing!

- Make sure the vase is clean and dry.
- Think about what sort of pattern you want to make.
- Attach the beads using strong glue; we used contact glue, which can be used on glass among other things.
- Allow to dry completely before adding fresh flowers to the vase.

A vase and beads/mosaic are all the materials you need.

Attach the beads using transparent contact glue in the pattern you want. We made a flower pattern on our vase.

The vase was so pretty that we almost didn't need to add any flowers, but it looked just as good with some flowers in it.

A COOL *Concrete Ball*

A really cool ball made of concrete can be cast using a regular plastic soccer ball. Let your kids help you fill the ball with concrete to make a new, rock-hard ball. It looks great just sitting in the backyard. A great tip is to make several and place them in a row by a bush or alongside a pathway.

- Cut a hole or slit into a regular, smooth plastic ball using a box cutter.
- Mix the concrete according to the instructions on page 12.
- Fill the ball with concrete.
- Leave the concrete ball to dry for at least 24 hours; it should not be left in the sun.
- Remove the concrete ball by cutting the plastic one.
- Use sandpaper to remove any rough bits around the area where the hole or slit was placed.

Cut a hole in a plastic ball with a box cutter.

Fill the ball with concrete; it can be a bit difficult to fill the whole thing.

Casting a concrete ball was a new project for us and it was more of a test to see how it would turn out than anything. We were positively surprised by the results and we think the concrete ball, with its beautiful round shape, is an asset to the garden. One side is flat, which is unavoidable, but that's not a bad thing.

We have a mixed bag of projects that all lead to wonderful and mostly useful things. Let your imagination run wild, grab a real egg, and make some fun Easter decorations from concrete. Or visit a thrift store and buy some cheap, mismatched porcelain that you can crush and make into your own mosaic to decorate concrete with. Guaranteed hours of fun!

Pretty Under THE POT

A fun project that mixes concrete and mosaic is pot holders. We made our mosaic from crushed porcelain that we placed in the wet concrete. The mold is a plastic candy box, and cheap porcelain can be bought at thrift stores. Then, all you need to do is go home and crush it into regular-sized pieces.

- Get a plastic mold, which can be either round or square. We used a candy box.
- To make mosaic from old porcelain, you crush it into small pieces. We bought small saucers that we wrapped in newspaper and crushed with a hammer. It really is a question of experimenting until you have the right amount of pieces.
- Brush the inside of the mold with vegetable oil.
- Mix the concrete according to the instructions on page 12.
- Pour the concrete into the mold; it should be around 1 ¼ inches (3 cm) thick.
- Carefully tap the mold against the ground a couple of times to remove any air bubbles.
- Gently tap or press the mosaic into the concrete.
- Leave the pot holder to dry for at least 24 hours. Make sure it is on a flat surface in a shady area.
- For the best results, water the concrete a couple of times while it's drying.
- Remove the pot holder from the mold.

Shards of crushed porcelain are carefully pressed or tapped into the wet concrete.

This mosaic is from blue patterned saucers, which make a great contrast with the gray concrete.

" Odd saucers with pretty patterns hardly cost a thing at the thrift stores. Buy as many as you can and go home and crush them to bits to use as mosaic. "

Candleholders

In our opinion, candles should be used a lot more often than just at parties. When fall comes and it starts to get dark, it is worth lighting some candles to welcome the family home after a long day. Concrete candleholders look a bit more exclusive and help avoid burn marks. Ours were decorated with round, smooth mosaic.

- You will need a candle, a small plastic bucket (we used an old container for sour cream from a restaurant), concrete, and if you wish, mosaic materials.
- Brush the bottom and partway up the inside of the bucket with vegetable oil.
- Wind some plastic wrap once around the candle to ensure that it will loosen from the concrete.
- Mix the concrete according to the instructions on page 12.
- Pour the concrete in the bucket; the amount will vary depending on how tall you want the holder to be; we made ours around 4 inches (10 cm) high.
- Gently tap the mold against the ground to remove any air bubbles.
- Press the torch into the concrete.
- Place some stones on the candle to keep it weighed down and prevent it from rising to the surface.
- Carefully press or tap the mosaic into the concrete.
- Leave the concrete to dry for at least 24 hours. Don't leave it in the sun.
- Water the concrete a few times while it's drying for the best results.
- Once the concrete is dry, carefully loosen the torch from the holder and remove the plastic wrap. Put the candle back into the holder.

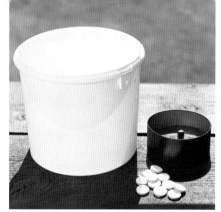

This bucket is the right size and is actually from a restaurant. They'll often give you old packaging if you ask for it.

The concrete and candle have been added to the bucket. If you want to decorate with mosaic, you just need to carefully press or tap the pieces into the wet concrete before leaving it to dry for 24 hours.

Brighten up the dark fall nights. These candle-holders can be left outside; you just need to replace the candles once they burn out.

An Herb Pot

It's easy to make a nice pot for fresh herbs; the materials cost next to nothing but the result looks professional. Place one or more on the kitchen counter or windowsill for an eye-catching display. A pot with some herbs in it also makes a lovely gift instead of flowers.

- For the mold you can use a large paper cup, for example, a large take-out coffee cup. In order to make it a pot, you need a second mold to press into the concrete; a white disposable plastic cup works perfectly.
- Brush the inside of the larger paper cup and the outside of the smaller cup with vegetable oil.
- Mix the concrete according to the instructions on page 12.
- Add the concrete to the paper cup but don't fill it all the way up, as there needs to be space to press the plastic cup into it without the concrete overflowing.
- Carefully tap the cup against the ground to remove any air bubbles.
- Press the smaller plastic cup into the concrete.
- Carefully tap the cups against the ground a few more times.
- Tape across the edges to stop the plastic cup from floating up.
- Leave the pot to dry for at least 24 hours.
- For the best result, water the concrete once during the drying time by spraying it with water.
- Carefully loosen the paper cup from the pot by simply pulling the cup apart at the seam and pulling it off.
- Carefully remove the plastic cup.
- Feel free to add felt furniture pads to the bottom to avoid scratches.
- The pot is finished.

A paper cup, a small plastic cup, and some tape.

The paper cup is filled with concrete and the plastic cup is pressed into it. The tape holds the plastic cup in place and stops it from floating up. It now needs to dry for 24 hours.

The plastic cup has left a pattern on the inside of the pot.

Our "coffee cup" pots are done and look great on a tray with herbs and oil. Just place it on the table once it's time to eat.

HARD "BOILED" *Eggs*

These cute little concrete eggs are harder than hardboiled ones and you can actually make them in real egg shells, which is a great alternative to painting eggs at Easter. Fill the empty egg shell with concrete and then, once it's dry, peel the egg. Then it's up to you to decide what to do with it; ours ended up on our table on top of some napkins.

- Make a little hole at the top of the egg.
- Empty the contents.
- Rinse the egg shell.
- Mix the concrete according to the instructions on page 12.
- Fill the egg with concrete; it's easiest if you place the egg in an egg cup.
- Gently knock the egg to get rid of any air bubbles.
- Leave the egg to dry for at least 24 hours.
- Peel off the egg shell.

With projects this small, you can easily mix the concrete in a little bowl with a spoon. Carefully fill the egg all the way up.

Leave the egg to dry for 24 hours before peeling off the shell.

Such a cute little table decoration. Why not let all the guests take their concrete eggs home after the party? We guarantee your guests will appreciate it.

THE CUTEST *Tray*

The cutest tray is the one you make yourself. You can easily pick up an old, worn tray, as well as an old saucer, at a thrift store. Pick and choose between the colors and patterns and choose a combination that works before crushing the porcelain. Tile adhesive/glue and grout are all you need to decorate the tray with mosaic. We chose to place an entire saucer in the middle of the tray and then decorated with mosaic pieces around it.

- Wash the tray and leave it to dry completely.
- Wrap the porcelain in some newspaper and place it on a durable surface. Use a hammer and bash it gently until you have pieces in your desired size.
- Place the pieces on the tray to see how the pattern works and then remove them.
- Brush some adhesive/glue with a tile adhesive comb. Adhesive can be found in home improvement or craft stores as well as at tile specialists.
- Press the porcelain pieces into the adhesive in the pattern of your choice. If you want to make the one that we did, press a small saucer in the middle.
- Leave to dry.
- Once dry it's time to grout; we used white grouting. Mix the grout according to the instructions and smooth the grout over the mosaic with a grout spreader. Remove excess grout with a damp sponge.
- When everything is dry, polish it with a dry cloth.
- The tray is ready to use.

After checking out some thrift stores, we returned home with a tray and some saucers. The tray made of tin is perfect to dress with shards from the crushed saucers.

Tile adhesive/glue is spread over the tray with an adhesive comb.

Now it's time to make a unique pattern with the porcelain shards.

We're very proud of all this fun handiwork that resulted in our cute tray.

Button holder

A bunch of buttons are given a whole new spark of life, and they are adorable when combined with concrete. Bags of mixed buttons can be bought in craft stores. A small concrete flowerpot was decorated with colorful buttons of varying sizes.

- For the pot you will need two plastic pots, a large one and a slightly smaller one.
- Sometimes the pots you buy in stores have holes in the bottom, so they will need to be taped over to prevent the concrete from leaking out.
- Brush the inside of the large pot and the outside of the smaller pot with vegetable oil.
- Mix the concrete according to the description on page 12.
- Pour the concrete into the large pot but leave a gap at the top, as you need to press the small pot into the concrete.
- Gently tap the pot against the ground to get rid of any air bubbles.
- Press the smaller pot into the concrete.
- Gently tap the pot against the ground again.
- Hold the small pot down and decorate the edge with buttons by tapping or pressing them gently into the concrete.
- Place a weight on the small pot to stop it from floating up. A water-filled plastic bottle is perfect to place inside the pot.
- Leave the pot to dry for at least 24 hours.
- To get the best results, water the concrete once during the drying process by spraying some water on it.
- Carefully loosen both plastic pots from the concrete pot and plant a pretty flower in your brand new pot.

This pot is as cute as a button!

"Don't forget that buttons are an alternative to mosaic tiles."

The buttons remind us of a bag of colorful candy.

Brushing the molds with vegetable oil makes them easier to remove from the concrete.

Press or tap the buttons lightly into the concrete around the edge of the plant pot.

When the concrete is completely dry, it turns a lovely light gray color, which looks great against the colorful buttons.

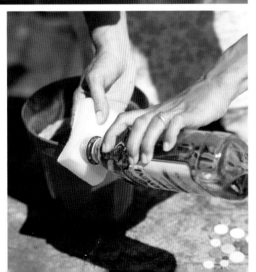

Pleated

When we made these small pots with pleats, we were pleasantly surprised by the results. They were perfect; the edge was even and thin and the pleats were razor sharp. The pleated pots we used for our molds were made of the cheapest plastic ones we could find in the grocery store—which is a bonus, along with the fact that you can reuse them.

- Two pleated plastic pots are needed to make one concrete pot.
- Paint the inside of one pot and the outside of the other with vegetable oil.
- Mix the concrete according to the instructions on page 12.
- Fill the pot that's been greased on the inside with concrete, but leave space at the top to allow for the other pot to be pressed inside without spilling over.
- Gently tap the pot against the ground a few times to remove any air bubbles.
- Press the second pot into the concrete.
- Gently tap the pots against the ground a few more times.
- Tape together with two strong bits of tape to ensure the pot stays in place and doesn't float to the top.
- Leave the pot to dry for at least 24 hours.
- For the best result, water the concrete once while it's drying by spraying it with some water.
- Carefully loosen the plastic pots from the concrete.
- If need be, smooth the edges with some fine sandpaper to make it nice and even.

These small pleated pots look great when grouped together and work just as well inside or outside.

The pot should be filled halfway up with concrete to allow space for the second pot to be pressed into it.

Wide masking tape holds the second pot in place while it sets for at least 24 hours.

> "We are still surprised at how smooth and level the concrete becomes once it's set and removed from the mold."

Outstanding results in our opinion—lovely smooth and level concrete with razor-sharp edges.

A MOSAIC *H*

Letters are always popular when it comes to interior design and there are many different styles, with wood and metal being the most usual. We were inspired by this and created a mosaic letter. The letter looks great as a decorative piece and works just as well on a door, such as one in a child's nursery. A large H made from strong cardboard from the craft store acted as our frame. Then we used glass mosaic to cover the letter.

- Test your pattern first by placing the mosaic on the letter and ensure that the measurements and color combinations work.
- Spread tile adhesive/glue on the letter with a tile adhesive comb. It's best to do one side at a time. The adhesive/glue can be bought at a home improvement or craft store or at a tile specialist.
- Add the mosaic by pressing it on.
- When everything is dry, you need to add the grout. We used white grout and mixed it according to the instructions on the packaging.
- Spread the grout over the mosaic with a grout spreader and remove any excess with a damp sponge.
- When everything is dry, polish the surface with a dry cloth.

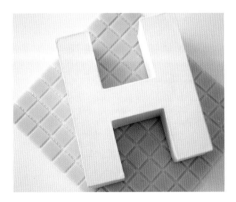

The letter H made from cardboard is from a craft store and the mosaic is made of normal, traditional glass mosaic materials.

Place the mosaic pieces on the H, making sure the measurements work before you glue them down. Spread some tile adhesive on the letter with a tile adhesive comb, a bit at a time, and add the mosaic pieces.

Almost the entire letter is dressed in mosaic and needs to be completely dry before you start grouting.

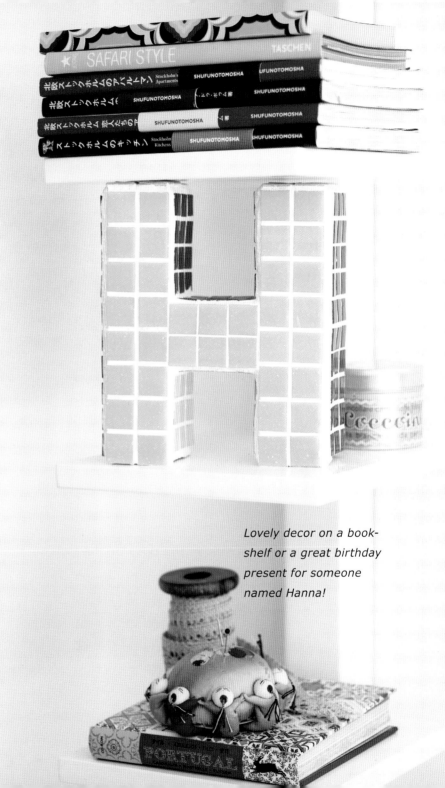

Lovely decor on a bookshelf or a great birthday present for someone named Hanna!

Our projects labeled "intermediate" require a bit more time and effort but they aren't especially complicated. You might need to make a mold from particleboard and joists to make a tabletop or a top for a concrete TV stand. In this chapter, we will also give you tips on how to create patterns in concrete with wallpaper, rubber flooring, and tablecloths, and we will really be indulging in tiles and mosaic! So pull some old objects out from storage and give them a new spark of life with mosaic. They will end up as new and unique works of art.

Concrete TABLETOP

A really cool table for the porch or backyard can be made from concrete. You will also need a frame of some kind, as only the tabletop will be made from concrete. How the tabletop is attached to the frame depends on the frame's shape, but usually it's enough to place the tabletop on top of the frame. If you need to, you can drill into the concrete and secure it with screws.

We used a bit of rubber flooring to make the tabletop's spotty pattern, but it's up to you whether you choose a patterned or smooth table. In order to avoid making the tabletop too heavy, we used two sorts of concrete: regular fine concrete and a lightweight concrete mixed with Styrofoam.

A great looking and durable table for the backyard. The frame is from an old Ikea outdoor table, which was great to use as a base for the concrete top. French metal chairs worked perfectly with the new concrete table.

A touch of romanticism with this pretty bunch of flowers makes a great contrast to the hard concrete.

- The mold for the tabletop is made from particleboard and joists.
- Measure and screw together the joists in the size required.
- Screw the joists onto the particleboard.
- Place the rubber floor into the mold with the pattern facing up.
- In order to make the tabletop durable, it needs to be reinforced. You can buy reinforcing net at a home improvement center where they will cut it to your required size.
- Mix the fine concrete according to the instructions on page 12.
- Pour the fine concrete into the mold so that the whole mold is covered with an approximately 1 ¼ inch (3 cm) deep layer.
- Gently tap the mold against the ground a few times to get rid of any air bubbles, as this will make your surface smooth and enhance the pattern.
- Mix the light concrete in the same way as you mixed the fine concrete.
- Fill up the mold with the light concrete.
- Press the reinforcement into the concrete so that it is covered by the concrete.
- Gently tap the mold against the ground again to remove any remaining air bubbles.
- Leave the tabletop to dry for at least 24 hours, making sure it is on a flat surface and not in the sun.
- For the best results, water the concrete a few times while it's drying.
- Carefully pry the tabletop from the mold.
- Attach or place the tabletop on the frame or screw some legs onto it.

The mold is ready to use. The joists have been screwed together to form a rectangle that has been screwed onto the particleboard. The measurements were adjusted according to the size of the rubber mat placed in the mold with the pattern facing up.

The mold has been filled up, first with the fine concrete and then the light concrete. The reinforcement is then pressed into the concrete.

The rubber flooring's spotted pattern makes the tabletop spotty as well.

A MARVELOUS *Mailbox*

Make your mailbox something that will catch the eye of any passersby. By covering it in tiles or mosaic you create a mailbox with a personal touch that you can be proud of. It's a fun way to change a basic item into something unique. We have used our favorite tiles—wonderfully patterned tiles from India that can be bought individually. One tile was all we needed and we paired it with two plain tiles in two different colors. Looks great, doesn't it?

- You need a basic mailbox, old or new.
- Make sure it's clean and dry.
- Plan your pattern and test it by placing the tiles and mosaic on the mailbox. To make it easier we only covered the front.
- Spread tile adhesive/glue over the mailbox with a tile adhesive comb.
- Tile adhesive/glue can be found at home improvement stores, in craft stores, or at a tile specialist.
- Place the tile/mosaic where you want it.
- Leave it to dry.
- The last bit is adding the grout; we used white grouting for tiles. Mix the grout according to the instructions on the packaging and spread over the tiles/mosaic with a grout spreader. Remove any excess with a damp sponge.
- Once dry, polish the surface with a dry cloth.
- Now run outside and put up your new mailbox!

It's a pleasure to go out and get the mail.

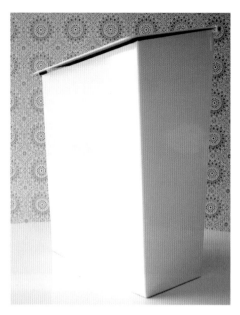

We started off with a basic standard mailbox.

Start off by designing a pattern and test the pieces on the box to ensure that your measurements work.

Spread tile adhesive/glue on the mailbox with a tile adhesive comb. Tile adhesive/glue can be found at the home improvement center, at the craft store, or at tile specialists.

Place the tiles/mosaic and gently press down.

The grout has dried and the mailbox is in its place.

Our favorite tiles come from India and have the most wonderful, colorful patterns. Sometimes the tiles are old and have been used in another project before being removed and shipped to Sweden, which is pretty neat.

Three concrete pictures in a row is both hip and impressive.

Heavy WALLS

Hanging three concrete pictures on the wall looks really striking. It's better to make several smaller pictures than to make one big one due to the weight. We made our three pictures at the same time. The pattern was made using structured wallpaper and the tiles were from a French antique market, making these pictures extra special.

- Make a mold in three parts out of particleboard and joists from a home improvement store.
- Measure and screw the joists together to create three equal sized squares.
- Screw the joists to the particleboard.
- Cut a piece of wallpaper with a structured pattern.
- Put a piece of wallpaper in each mold with the pattern facing up. The wallpaper should go up over the edges so that they too become patterned.
- Place double-sided tape (carpet tape) on the front of the tile so it covers the whole tile but not the edges. This ensures that the tile stays in place but is kept clean of concrete.
- Slightly moisten the tiles so they don't absorb too much water from the concrete.
- Place the tiles in the molds, front facing down.
- Cut a piece of chicken wire to reinforce it.
- Mix the concrete according to the instructions on page 12.
- Pour the concrete into the three molds.
- Gently tap the molds on the ground a few times to remove any air bubbles.
- Reinforce the picture by pressing chicken wire into the concrete.
- Gently tap the mold against the ground again.
- Press a picture hook into the concrete on each picture.
- Leave the pictures to set for at least 24 hours. Make sure they are left on a flat surface and not in the sun.
- For the best result, water the concrete a few times while it's drying.
- Carefully remove the pictures from the molds by gently prying them loose.
- Pull the double-sided tape off the tiles.
- Hang your work of art in a group on the wall.

The material required to make this concrete picture include some particleboard, joists, wallpaper, tiles, and picture hooks (as well as concrete, of course).

The wallpaper needs to have a raised pattern with a plastic feel, as this gives the concrete a great pattern. The wallpaper should not have a fabric surface, as the concrete will stick to this. We found our wallpaper in a homeware store.

The joists are in place and create three separate molds. The pieces of wallpaper are lying with the pattern facing up and go up over the edges, while the tiles are in place with double–sided tape.

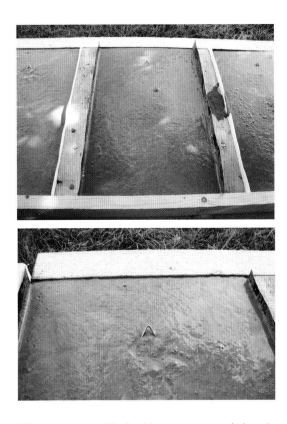

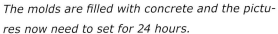

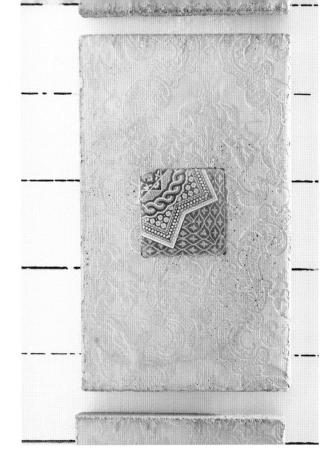

The molds are filled with concrete and the pictures now need to set for 24 hours.

A picture hook makes it easy to hang the picture on the wall, as it is cast into the concrete.

These worn, old tiles from a French antique market were finally put to good use.

You can clearly see the lovely pattern that has been left in the concrete from the wallpaper; pretty neat, isn't it?

A CUTE *Chair*

A chair is a great alternative to a traditional bedside table, especially if you dress the seat with mosaic patterns. We transformed a wooden chair from Ikea into a decorative and fun bedside table that is completely unique!

We started by painting the chair white with furniture paint, as this enhances the mosaic.

Then we used a glass mosaic with an irregular shape from the craft store.

We matched the mosaic with the rest of the décor and textiles in the bedroom.

- Paint the whole chair, except the seat, white and leave to dry.
- Test your pattern by placing the mosaic on the seat in the pattern you want. You can also sketch the pattern on a piece of paper.
- Spread the tile adhesive/glue on the seat with a tile adhesive comb. The adhesive can be found at a home improvement center, in craft stores, or at a tile specialist.
- Place the mosaic on the chair.
- Leave to dry.
- Mix the grout according to the instructions on the packaging and spread over the tiles/mosaic with a grout spreader.
- Remove any excess grout with a damp sponge.
- When it's dry, polish the surface with a dry cloth.
- Find a spot for your new piece of furniture.

A basic kitchen chair was the starting point for this project.

The new chair works really well as a bedside table and is also fairly easy to make.

When the chair has been painted white and the color dried, it's time to spread the tile adhesive/glue onto the seat.

Place small, irregular pieces of mosaic made of glass over the seat.

Mix the grout according to the instructions on the packaging and spread over the tiles/mosaic with a grout spreader.

Patterns, PATTERNS, PATTERNS, PATTERNS

Giving the concrete a pattern is exciting because you can really experiment with it. It's all about trial and error. Not all of our projects have worked out, but sometimes we achieved excellent results, like with these four different patterns.

Here you can see close–ups of the patterns themselves in the concrete and you can use them on all sorts of things, such as tabletops as well as bowls, plant pots, and plates.

Textiles, plastic, paper, and rubber are great materials to get patterns from. Wallpaper with a plastic raised pattern is perfect but won't work if any part of the pattern is velvet, which you find with a lot of wallpaper. Like we said, you need to experiment, and you can start with getting some inspiration for things that will leave an imprint in the concrete here.

Patterns

"We have so many lace cloths stored away and we can finally make use of them."

- The basic principle here is to place the item that is giving the concrete its pattern at the bottom of the mold with the pattern facing up.
- If you are making a tabletop, make the mold out of particleboard and joists that you can get from a home improvement center.
- Measure and screw together the joists in your desired shape.
- Screw the joists onto the particleboard.
- Place the patterned material into the mold with the pattern facing up.
- Our example shows a piece of rubber flooring with dots, a lace runner made from plastic, a tablecloth and a piece of lace, and finally some wallpaper.
- In order for the table to be durable, it needs to be reinforced. You can get reinforcement mesh at the hardware store where they can cut it to the size you require (they have the right tools for this).
- Mix the concrete according to the instructions on page 12.
- Pour the concrete into the mold.
- Press the reinforcement into the concrete so it is completely covered by the concrete.
- Gently tap the mold against the ground a few times to get rid of any air bubbles, as this will give you a smooth surface and enhance the pattern.
- Leave it to set for at least 24 hours. Make sure it's on a flat surface and keep it out of the sun.
- For the best results, water the concrete a few times while it's drying.
- Loosen the concrete from the mold by gently prying it out.

This concrete project was decorated with a pretty pattern from lace. The variety of lace patterns you can experiment with are endless, which is lots of fun.

We sacrificed a tablecloth with a crocheted edge that we got from a thrift store and a piece of lace ribbon.

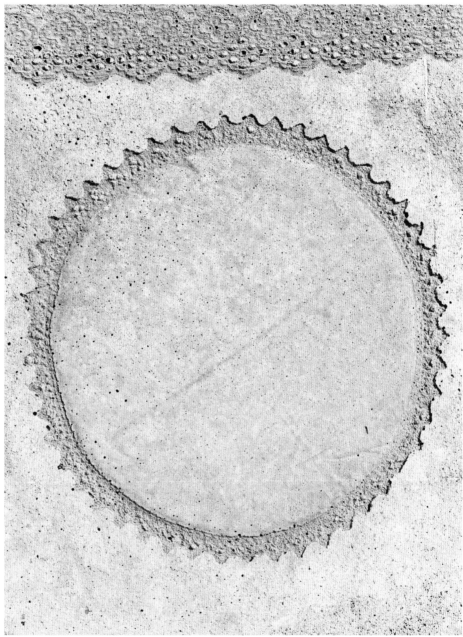

This tabletop was decorated with a small pattern. To create it we used a lace runner made of plastic from a homeware store.

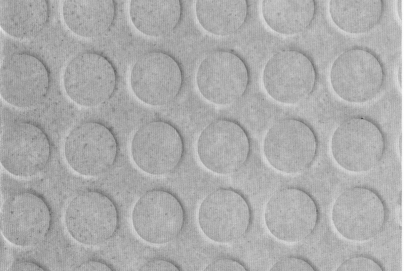

We created edgy spots from a patterned piece of rubber flooring. Search hardware stores for flooring or other materials that can create patterns. A picture of the rubber floor can be found on page 59.

This is probably our favorite: a perfect pattern with a soft shape in contrast to the hard concrete. A piece of wallpaper with a raised plastic pattern was perfect to cast in concrete.

"We were happy to discover that structured wallpaper casts a pattern in the concrete."

A PATTERNED THRIFT *Store Table*

This little table in our garage was just waiting for us to give it a new spark of life. When we had painted the frame bright green, we decided to place a kurbit–inspired pattern on the tabletop by using shards of tile. The inspiration came from a painted basket, which you can see in the picture. If you have something that inspires you, then you can try and make something similar, as long as you aren't disappointed if it doesn't look exactly the same!

- Break the tiles into pieces by placing them in a towel or several layers of newspaper and hit them with a hammer until you get the piece sizes you want.
- We used both shards from tiles as well as regular small pieces of mosaic.
- Clean the tabletop.
- Place the shards to test the pattern so you can get an idea of how it might look; take your time getting it the way you want.
- Spread the tile adhesive/glue onto the tabletop with a tile adhesive comb. The adhesive/glue can be found at a home improvement center, a craft store, or a tile specialist.
- Place the shards/mosaic in the correct place.
- Leave to dry.
- Mix the grout according to the instructions on the packaging and spread over the tiles/mosaic with a grout spreader. Remove any excess with a damp sponge.
- Once dry, polish with a dry cloth.
- Behold, your table!

In order to make a nice tabletop, you need tiles and some mosaic to combine it with (optional). You also need a hammer and a towel. Smash the tiles in the towel with the hammer until you have the right piece sizes you need.

We prefer white grout, but that is our preference. Here, we are grouting the surface to make sure it is nice and even.

Shards of tile and mosaic are laid out into a kurbit–inspired pattern. A tip is to mix a lot of white into the pattern to make it look pretty.

This small thrift store table has been given a new spark of life. The painted baskets gave us the inspiration for our pattern.

YOUR FAVORITE *Mirror*

This is our favorite mirror, whose vibrant colors and style inspired us to create many things, but most important of all, it gave us the idea of dressing a mirror with mosaic products and tiles. At thrift stores you can often find mirrors with old frames at a low price. The only requirement is that the frame needs to be smooth. Once you have found your frame you can choose what to dress it with—whether it's tiles, mosaic, shards, beads, or anything else, just let your creativity flow.

- Make sure the mirror frame is clean and dry.
- Place the mosaic, or whatever you are dressing the mirror with, out to make sure it works.
- Spread the adhesive/glue onto the frame with a tile adhesive comb. Adhesive/glue can be found at a home improvement center, craft store, or tile specialist.
- Add the mosaic.
- Leave to dry.
- Mix the grout according to the instructions on the packaging and spread it over the tiles/mosaic with a grout spreader. Wipe off any excess with a damp sponge.
- When everything is dry, polish the surface with a dry cloth.

This mirror is old and originally comes from India. We bought it in a shop specializing in Indian and Middle Eastern furniture. The frame is covered in wonderful strips made from colorful secondhand tiles.

We love this wonderful mirror. It has inspired many of our projects.

SEVERAL *Pots* IN ONE

Work with what you've got. We took a cardboard box that was not being used for anything and tried to cast concrete in it. After some deliberation, we decided to make a square pot containing several holes so that we could combine different flowers or herbs in it. We used regular plastic pots for the holes and decorated with a light pink tile. Just simple and cheap material, which yielded a pot of a different kind.

- Find a cardboard box or something similar, some plastic pots, and one or a few tiles.
- Place double-sided tape (carpet tape) on the front of the tile so it covers the whole tile but not the edges. This makes sure that the tile stays in place and is kept clean from concrete.
- Place the taped tile where you want it to sit on one of the cardboard walls.
- Mix the concrete according to the instructions on page 12.
- Pour the concrete into the cardboard box but not all the way up, as you need to be able to press down three plastic pots.
- Carefully tap the box against the ground a few times to remove any air bubbles.
- Press the plastic pots into the concrete.
- To avoid the pots floating to the surface you can use a strong tape over the cardboard to keep them in place.
- Leave the concrete to dry for at least 24 hours. Make sure the box is on a flat surface and not in the sun.
- For the best result, water the concrete a few times during the drying time.
- Loosen the box from the concrete and remove the double-sided tape from the tile.
- Sort herbs and flowers into a lovely arrangement to place in the pots.

A project to be really proud of.

All you need is a cardboard box, some plastic pots, and a few tiles.

Place double-sided tape on the front of the tiles so that it covers the tile but not the edges; this keeps the tile in place and prevents any concrete from getting on it. Place the taped tile on one of the box's walls.

When the box is filled with concrete and the pots are in place, tape across the box to keep the pots from floating up.

Several pots in one is perfect for growing herbs on the kitchen counter.

"As much as we can, we try to use molds that cost next to nothing, or even better, free!"

CONCRETE FOR THE *TV*

Concrete surfaces can be used in many different ways, and we thought it would be a fun idea to cast a TV stand. The type of frame you use is not important; it can be placed on a set of legs or on top of a bench or, like in this example, a cupboard. The basic method is the same: place a concrete top on a frame before adding your television to it. For this project we made the top pattern by using structured wallpaper.

- The mold is made from particleboard and joists from the home improvement store.
- Measure and screw the joists together in the shape you want.
- Screw the joists to the particleboard.
- Cut the wallpaper to size; this should be structured wallpaper, as in a wallpaper with a raised, plastic pattern.
- Place the wallpaper in the mold with the pattern facing up and the wallpaper going up over the edges so that the tabletop will be patterned all over and so that the edges get a curved shape.
- In order to make the top durable, it needs to be reinforced; chicken wire works well and is easy to cut.
- Cut the chicken wire to fit the mold.
- Mix the concrete according to the instructions on page 12.
- Pour the concrete into the mold on top of the wallpaper in a roughly 2 inch (5 cm) thick layer.
- Gently tap the mold against the ground a few times to get rid of any air bubbles and to ensure that the surface is smooth.
- Press the reinforcement into the concrete so that it is covered by the concrete.
- Gently tap the mold a few more times against the ground to remove any air bubbles.
- Leave the concrete to dry for at least 24 hours. Make sure the surface is flat and not in sunlight.
- For the best result, water the concrete a few times during the drying time.
- Gently pry the concrete from the mold.
- Place the top onto a bench or the equivalent and add your TV.

Tough TV style.

The cupboard that the TV was on was given a new spark of life with a concrete top.

The mold is made from particleboard and joists. Wallpaper is used to give the top a pattern.

The wallpaper needs to be structured with a raised, plastic pattern.

Place the wallpaper in the mold with the pattern facing up. It should cover the edges too.

74

You can clearly see the
pattern from the wallpa-
per here and the surface
of the concrete was as
smooth as silk.

YOUR FAVORITE *Sofa*

This is another favorite. Just like the mirror on page 66, this one has inspired us a great deal. With its worn, shabby look and wonderful turquoise color and beautiful tiles, it gives us energy and inspires us. This sofa looks so good that we created a whole layout with the sofa as the focal point.

What we want to convey is that you can simply place a single tile on furniture, walls, doors, and many other unusual things. So once you have found your favorite tiles, make sure you buy several and find a spot to put them.

- The surface where the tile is being placed needs to be clean and dry.
- Spread some tile adhesive/glue in place with a tile adhesive comb. Adhesive/glue can be found at the home improvement center, craft stores, or a tile specialist.
- Press the tile in place.
- Finished!

Our unique sofa is from a shop specializing in Indian furniture.

This whole room is based around the sofa. The décor made with tiles gives it character.

The next section contains our most advanced projects, but don't let that scare you, as they are really not that difficult. As long as you have time to spare and aren't afraid of experimenting, you can create anything from stairs to a stylish bedside table.

In some projects we use form plywood, which is made especially for casting with concrete. Form plywood releases easily from the concrete and the surface is left nice and smooth. It is more expensive than regular particleboard, but it can be worth that extra price when making more advanced projects.

A PERFECT *Porch*

If you want to create a unique patio, you can make lovely concrete tiles. It does take some time, as you will need to make several, but once you have made one, the rest will be easier—a sort of concrete production line. We chose to decorate our tiles with a patterned Moroccan ceramic tile, which really does give it that little extra something. If you can, make three molds at the same time so you can make three tiles at once. To make the tiles durable, you should reinforce them. You can use reinforcement mesh or chicken wire.

"We never tire of patterned, Moroccan ceramic tiles."

We settled on nine tiles for this porch area, which is the crowning jewel in our garden.

- The molds for the tiles are made from form plywood and joists that can be bought at the home improvement center.
- Measure and screw the joists together into the size you need. Our joists measured 16 x 16 inches (40 x 40 cm) and we made three at the same time.
- Screw the joists onto the form plywood.
- Place double-sided tape (carpet tape) onto the front of the tiles so that the tape covers the tile but not the edges. This keeps the tile in place and clean of concrete.
- Moisten the tiles so that they don't soak up too much water from the concrete.
- Place the ceramic tiles in place, one in each mold, back facing up.
- In order to make the tiles durable, they should be reinforced. Reinforcement mesh or chicken wire can be purchased at a home improvement center. The reinforcement mesh needs to be cut to the right size at the store, as they have the right tools there.
- Mix the concrete according to the instructions on page 12.
- Pour the concrete into the molds.
- Gently tap the molds against the ground a few times to remove any air bubbles.
- Press the reinforcement mesh into the concrete, ensuring it is completely covered.
- Gently tap the molds against the ground again to remove any remaining air bubbles.
- Leave the tiles to dry for at least 24 hours. Make sure they are on a flat surface in the shade.
- For the best results, water the concrete a few times while it is drying.
- Carefully pry the concrete from the mold.
- Dig out an area in the ground and place the tiles where you want them.

The mold has a measurement of around 16 x 16 inches (40 x 40 cm) and is ready to be used. The ceramic tile with its taped front is in place with the back facing up, and now it's time to pour in the concrete and place the reinforcement in it.

We think the result looks great. Moroccan ceramic tiles have very beautiful patterns and look great when mixed together.

Furniture made from concrete is something most people only dream about, as many stores stock great concrete furniture but often with a high price tag to match. We hope you will dare to make your own concrete furniture. Start off by being inspired by our little bedside table that made a great addition to this bedroom. It is easy to make but you have to be accurate with the measurements when you make the mold. You can choose the size and shape yourself, but the two molds must be the same, one large and one small. The concrete is poured between the two molds.

- The mold for the table is made from form plywood.
- Measure and saw all the pieces for the mold.
- The mold consists of two sections, one smaller and one larger piece, as well as a flat piece for the base. In total you need 17 pieces.
- Screw together the pieces, one at a time. We recommend brackets to enable you to reach the screws when it's time to remove the mold.
- Place a strip of latex grout in the seams to seal it and to make the edges even.
- Place the smaller mold inside the larger one and measure carefully so that the distance between the two molds is equal all around; we had a distance of 1 ½ inches (4 cm).
- Screw both bits onto the base. Alternatively you can place a heavy weight on top of them to keep them from moving.
- Mix the concrete according to the instructions on page 12.
- Fill with concrete between the molds, all the way up to the edge.
- Tap the mold gently with a hammer to get rid of any air bubbles.
- Leave the concrete to dry for around 48 hours. Make sure the mold is on a flat surface and away from the sun.
- Carefully remove the bedside table from the mold by removing the screws and removing each section one by one. It can be a bit fiddly, so you need to be persistent.
- You can now be immensely proud of your very own piece of concrete furniture.

Finally finished: a very unique and practical bedside table, which adds character to your bedroom.

A larger mold and a smaller mold are both placed on the base ready to go. The distance between the two molds needs to be exactly the same all around.

It is worth placing a strip of latex grout in all the corners to keep it from leaking. It is also worth putting brackets in the corners of the inner mold so you can easily reach the screws when it's time to remove it.

Pour concrete between the molds, all the way up to the edges.

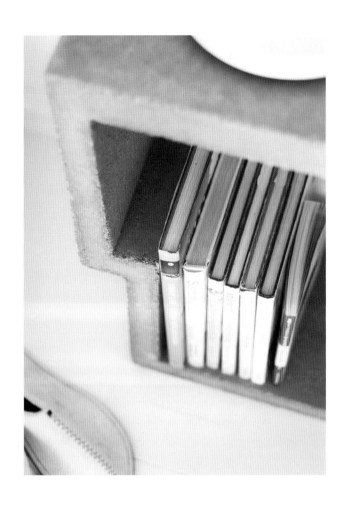

The bedside table has lots of space for books you want to keep close at hand.

Patterned STAIRS

Here we've made a new set of steps for an existing staircase. The old steps were removed and the new ones took their place; the measurements were adapted for the size of the staircase. It is important to reinforce the steps properly, so we recommend that you ask for advice from staff at a home improvement center to make sure you get the right size reinforcement based on the measurements you have, as all stairs are different. You can either make a mold and cast one step at a time or make several molds and cast several at the same time. To make patterns on the steps we used some stucco molding made from Styrofoam that we got at a home improvement center.

- Make a mold for the steps using form plywood and joists purchased from a home improvement center.
- Measure and screw together the joists in the size you need.
- Screw the joists onto the form plywood.
- Measure and saw the Styrofoam molding using a miter saw and place the pieces in the mold.
- Screw the Styrofoam to the mold so it stays in place and put a strip of latex grout along the seams to give you even corners.
- Brush the Styrofoam molding with vegetable oil.
- In order to make the steps durable, they need to be reinforced. You can get reinforcement mesh at the home improvement center where you can also get it cut to the right measurements. Ask the staff what type of reinforcement you need and how much to fit your steps.
- Mix the concrete according to the instructions on page 12. (Continued on the next page.)

The newly cast step is both decorative and highly individualistic.

- Pour the concrete into the mold.
- Tap the mold carefully against the ground a few times to remove any air bubbles, or tap with a hammer around the edges to vibrate the mold.
- Place the reinforcement into the concrete. It is important that it lands in the middle of the concrete to ensure it remains durable.
- Tap the mold carefully against the ground a few times to remove any air bubbles or tap a hammer around the edges a few more times to vibrate it after you have added the reinforcement.
- Cover the mold with plastic.
- Leave the step to dry for around 48 hours. Make sure it is on a flat surface and not in the sun.
- For the best result, water the concrete a few times while it is drying.
- Carefully pry the step from the mold to remove it.
- Add the steps one at a time until the staircase is complete.

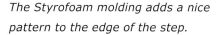

The Styrofoam molding adds a nice pattern to the edge of the step.

The mold for the step is ready to use; the joists have been screwed together to the right size and then screwed onto the form plywood. The Styrofoam molding is screwed onto the mold.

The Styrofoam molding is cut into pieces using a miter saw. We added a strip of latex grout to make sure the edges are even. The molding is painted with some vegetable oil to make it easier to remove from the concrete.

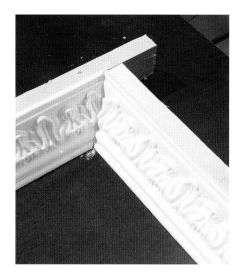

The mold is filled with concrete all the way up to the edge.

All the steps are in place and we have created an entirely new entrance.

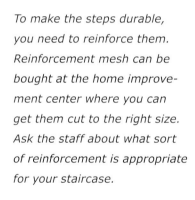

Gently tap the mold against the ground a few times to remove any air bubbles or vibrate the mold by tapping it with a hammer all the way around the edges.

To make the steps durable, you need to reinforce them. Reinforcement mesh can be bought at the home improvement center where you can get them cut to the right size. Ask the staff about what sort of reinforcement is appropriate for your staircase.

Place the reinforcement into the concrete, making sure it lands in the center to give it the best durability.

Cover the mold in plastic to make sure the concrete doesn't dry too fast.

A PROFESSIONAL *Pot on a Stand*

We wanted to make a pot on a stand and wondered how to best go about this. After a trip into town, we returned home with a plastic pot on a stand that could be separated into two parts. We decided to also cast our concrete pot in two parts that would then be glued together. The result exceeded our expectations and we ended up with a magnificent creation to plant our flowers in.

- You need a two-part plastic pot on a stand as well as two regular plastic buckets.
- Separate the pot into two parts.
- The top part of the pot is placed in a bucket, giving it some support and allowing it to stand up.
- Turn the stand upside down and make sure it's steady.
- Brush the inside of the top part and the inside of the upside down stand with vegetable oil.
- Mix the concrete according to the instructions on page 12.
- Pour the concrete in the upside down stand, all the way to the top.
- Pour the concrete in the top part that is in the bucket but leave some space at the top, as you need space to press down the second bucket.
- Gently tap both molds against the ground a few times to remove any air bubbles.
- Press the second bucket into the wet concrete at the top part of the pot to create a "hole," making a pot as opposed to just a lump of concrete.
- Place a heavy weight in the bucket to stop it from floating up.
- Leave the concrete to dry for at least 24 hours. Don't leave it in the sun.
- Gently pry the concrete from the mold; you might need to cut the plastic pot to remove the concrete.
- You are now left with two pieces that need to be glued together.
- Glue the foot to the top part of the pot with some heavy duty glue, for example PL 400.
- Plant some flowers and enjoy.

*This plant pot on a
stand is a magnificently
eye-catching addition
to your backyard.*

This is the plastic pot on a stand that we used as a mold for our concrete pot. We were able to separate it into two parts.

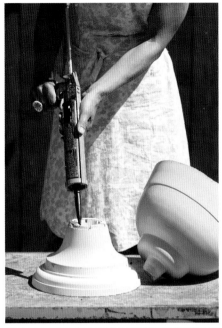

The two concrete parts now need to be joined together using some strong glue.

The stand was easy to cast, as it could be turned upside down and filled with concrete. The top part was placed in a bucket to keep it steady and then also filled with concrete. We left space at the top in order to be able to press the second bucket into it.

The pieces fit perfectly, as they have been cast according to the exact measurements of the original pot.

A LOVELY SQUARE *Birdbath*

Birdbaths are classics when it comes to casting in concrete. They can be made in so many different shapes and sizes. For this project we made a square birdbath decorated with a Moroccan ceramic tile at the bottom. As you are making your own mold for this bath, you can adapt the measurements after your own requirements.

You can of course skip the ceramic tile and make the birdbath purely concrete. To make the hole we used a thick piece of Styrofoam.

The ceramic tile was pressed into the concrete with the front taped onto the Styrofoam, which leaves it the right way up when the Styrofoam is removed.

- The mold for the birdbath is made from particleboard and joists that can be purchased in a home improvement center.
- You need a thick piece of Styrofoam, which can be bought at the same store.
- Measure and screw together the joists into the size that you require for the birdbath.
- Screw the frame made from the joists onto the particleboard.
- Add a strip of latex grout to the edges to seal it.
- Cut the Styrofoam so that it is around 1 ½ inches (4 cm) smaller than the mold.
- Brush the Styrofoam with vegetable oil (you don't need to cover the top side as that won't be covered by concrete).
- Place double-sided tape (carpet tape) on the front of the ceramic tile so that it covers the whole tile but not the sides. This keeps the tile in place but clean from concrete.
- Slightly moisten the tile so it doesn't absorb too much water from the concrete.
- Place the tile on the Styrofoam in the middle with the back facing up.
- Mix the concrete according to the instructions on page 12.
- Pour the concrete in the mold so that roughly half the mold is full. There needs to be space to add the Styrofoam board.
- Gently tap the mold against the ground a few times to remove any air bubbles.
- Press the Styrofoam board with the ceramic tile facing down into the concrete.
- To stop the Styrofoam from floating up, place a plank across that can be screwed or nailed onto the mold.
- Leave the birdbath to dry for at least 24 hours. Make sure it is on a flat surface in the shade.
- For the best results, water the concrete a few times while it is drying.
- Remove the birdbath from the mold as well as the piece of Styrofoam.
- Fill it with water and add some flowers and let the birds enjoy their bath.

Place double-sided tape on the front of the tile but not the edges. This keeps it in place.

The mold is ready and the Styrofoam has been cut to the right size and the tile has been added. It's now time to pour in the concrete.

Fill the mold halfway with concrete, leaving space to add the Styrofoam.

Seal the corners of the mold with some latex grout.

Place the Styrofoam in the concrete with the tile facing down.

Screw the plank to the edges of the mold to keep the Styrofoam in place.

Here's the finished result, which can be hard to visualize while you are working on it. The Styrofoam created a square "hole," turning it into a birdbath.

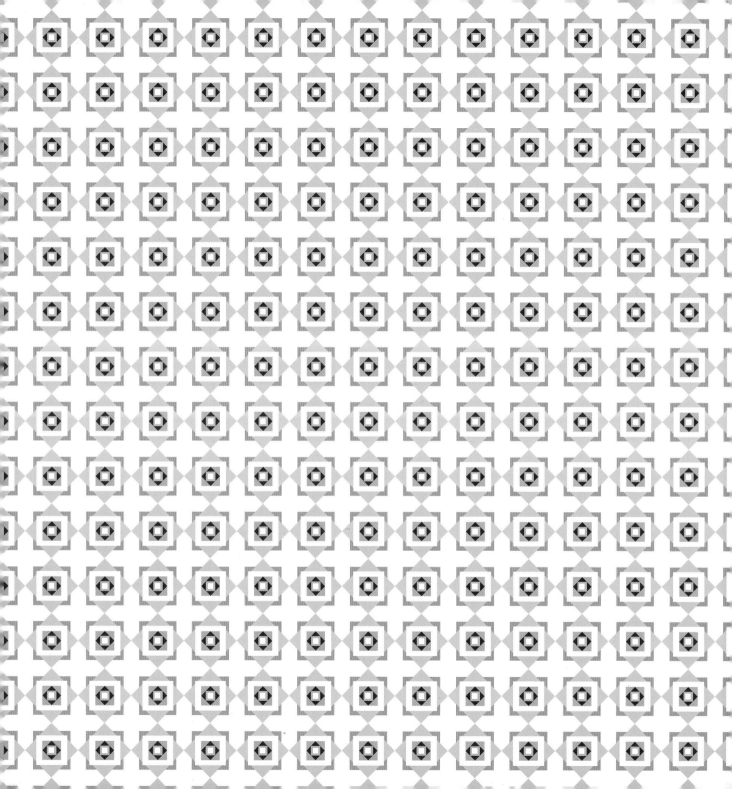